THE CAFÉ OF OUR DEPARTURE

PRISCILLA ATKINS

SIBLING RIVALRY PRESS
LITTLE ROCK, ARKANSAS
WWW.SIBLINGRIVALRYPRESS.COM

Sibling Rivalry Press, LLC
PO Box 26147
Little Rock, AR 72221
info@siblingrivalrypress.com

www.siblingrivalrypress.com

ISBN: 978-1-937420-87-1

Library of Congress Control Number: 2014959471

First Sibling Rivalry Press Edition, March 2015

For Lynn Drickamer
& Marylee Dalton

I.

II.

III.

Acknowledgments & Notes

. . . the smell of juniper
Where my dead best friend will always walk
beside me, stride ahead of me.
"When I walk with you, all I see is the heels
of your sneakers": were
You buried in your sneakers? Of course not,
though in a tender joke you were . . .

—James Schuyler
"The Morning of the Poem"

I.

Unguided Tour of Grief with Green Wallpaper

I want to get there first
I want to be there waiting
I want to weep
to dry my eyes
and order espresso
(your drink, not mine)
I want the black and white
I want the miniature
and the William Morris
willow wallpaper
I want the stairwell
of your last apartment
I want to toast high ceilings
and late weekend mornings
I want you there
I want to be alone

I want the restaurant almost filled
and you to be there
in another room
(I want you to have waited)
I want the day to change
from sun to clouds and then to rain
I want our laughter
and to be alone
I want a bamboo table
and an embroidered cloth
I want blue ink and Chinese paper
I want hunger
I want extra froth
and the tiny spoon

I want the alone
of the sarcophagus
I want the museum's silver hour
the green and gold
I want the eye and nose
and the background murmur
I want the bronze air
and the marble floor
I want to willow
I want to lie down
I want

POOF

I like sitting more than anything.
Last night I perched on the edge of the bed,
pulled up my left leg, rested the heel
on the mattress, and clipped the tiny nails
with one of those evil-looking clippers.
Then I did the other one.
Three weeks ago I went on a trip.
When I am at work, I notice the sound
of liquid pouring on the other side
of the partition.
Six, seven times a day, another glass.
Every afternoon I walk down to the mailbox
to get the mail. Well, not Sundays—
but, by accident, some holidays.
Then I feel foolish
and go back inside.
Most every morning I kiss Dean; we sit
and check out the beech trees,
whether or not anything special's
on the feeder.
Every day, there is this woman—me/not me—
getting dressed, sitting down, resting chin
on palm, turning over leaves
in her datebook, as if 12:20 p.m., Friday
September 17, 2004 never happened. As if
she never stood to pick up
the phone, never heard
Mark's words,
"He left a letter."
As if, any day—*poof!*—you will return.

CABINET OF WONDER

Embryo

Creepily irresistible, the corpse of the baby
crocodile, suspended inside his glass jar, grins.

Had I known what was in the cupboard
would I have opened it? Might I have avoided

the exhibit altogether? Then, I think how you always
took in everything. Were you here, you would march

right up, greet it eye-to-eye. The small
and the large of it. I lean in, note the claws

and scales, the tiny row of teeth overlapping
the jaw, think *serpent, dragon, magic.*

Resolves

I can will you to rise from the basement carpet where you
curled in your careful, last sleep. Your hands

gently untie the string and lift the plastic bag from your head;
the pills spill from your mouth like the apple from Snow

White's. You walk backwards up two flights until you are
in your second-floor kitchen and it is early morning. We

are drinking mugs of green tea, Chicago sun bouncing off
the linden filling your tall windows. Mark comes in

to kiss you as he leaves for work, and we wonder
what mischief we can conjure up—two forty-year-olds—

on this stolen day. What high hilarity can we find sniffing
your herbs in their rows of corked Erlenmeyer flasks.

Some horrific memory from high-school chemistry?
Or paging through the farewell issue of your favorite design

magazine, or your mother's church cookbook. The basement
exists in another universe. The bag floats under a shelf, the string

tucked and forgotten. But there, among the colorful porcelain
in your kitchen, I sense a darkness. Less than two weeks

since the last surgery, the tiny staples still track across
the top of your head. Strands of your hair caught

in those silver teeth, like they did at the hospital the last time
I saw you. I cannot avoid the utter weariness in your eyes.

My resolve weakens. I remember the lucid paragraphs of the letter
you left for us. And the image wavers. No, I will let you do

what you must do—what you have the right to do.
From my ghostly vantage point, one hundred and fifty miles

north, I will gasp, crumple, bite down hard, let the leafy
hours of night rub together as your shoulders gather weight.

Assertions

The first nights, hour of the wolf, I wake afraid, look at the clock:
always 3 a.m.

*

"If someone's going to get a brain tumor, the front left lobe
is the place to get it," my doctor friend emailed.
"Motor skills and other major functioning will not be
affected. Front-left controls *initiating* and *planning*."
I report this to you with a straight, cheerful face, two days after surgery.
You burst out laughing and slap the bedrail.

*

"What are you doing this weekend?" you asked, uncharacteristically,
two days before.
"Going to Detroit to visit Becky."

*

During the service, a young woman sings "Summertime."
Several people give eulogies. I read Cavafy.
Later, over wine and artichokes, one of your 150 friends teases me,
"I thought you might mention 'Ithaka' was read at Jackie O's funeral."
We decide a flashing sign, "This poem also read at Jackie O's funeral,"
would have added a certain *je-ne-sais-quoi.*
Another, now from San Francisco, stops me at the bar, asks if I remember
him—of course I do: the Thanksgiving dinner, his cat named Cheryl.

*

In your hospital room, I pointed to the speckled, magenta
blossoms in one of your bouquets and prodded you, once again,

for the name of that lily-like flower I can never remember.
"*Alstroemeria*," you say carefully, and hold my gaze in yours,
then add, "I know you're going to write a poem."

"Prince of the City"

Are you dancing among the tombstones at Graceland—did you find
the spot between the Palmers and the Pullmans where you took a piss
that sunny morning while I acted as the foil sipping coffee?

Maybe you're whipping down the Tuscan coast, chauffeuring Mark
to the airport—back to his job—before you return for another week,
poolside, at one of your wealthy friend's springtime villas.

Or, in a house of mirrors, are you dragging me, whining like a puppy,
to another contemporary art exhibit at Navy Pier?

Have you seen Paul? Is he healthy again? Did he get his pre-AIDS body back
like the angel promised?

Are you orbiting ceilings, considering possibilities for where you might
install shelving to display your Fiestaware?

Where you are I bet none of the chairs are more uncomfortable than your
narrow wicker dining room ones.

And none more comfortable than the velvety blue seats at the Goodman.

Are you browsing the store windows on Michigan Avenue,
catching the *Collection of Collections* at the Field,
studying maps at The Savvy Traveller?

This windy, autumn afternoon, the kind you loved, if I duck
into the café at the Hotel Burnham, drape one of their lush
linen napkins across my lap, order a white chocolate bread
pudding and two forks, will you come trotting through the door, late
as usual, your litany of excruciating excuses cracking me up just the same?

Hospitals & Guns

"They found a brain tumor," Mark phones.
Later, I piece the scene into a hard quilt:
a gurney, you lingering in a terrible tick-tock
of hours waiting for a room. (Doctors'
orders: "You can have a day to consider
which surgeon, but we will not release you
without the removal.") Long nights
of steroids messing with thoughts, with
sleep. Messing with life as you knew

it. Three weeks later, a seam across your head,
you're dead—pills and a plastic bag. After,
I dream us hostages: you at the wheel of
a strange car, masked man in the passenger seat
clasping a semi-automatic. You distract with
chatter ("This part of the city boasts big industry")
then—abrupt, smooth—you slam the brakes,
yank the gun, jump out, nosing it
to the sky—*bang!bang!bang!*—you save the day.

La Nature Morte

That last Friday, in the hospital, you held up the arts
section of *The Times* to show me the Met's

current spread of lush, detailed paintings—
Philippe Rousseau's "Still Life with Ham,"

De Heem's "Still Life with a Glass and Oysters."
Van Beyeren's "Still Life with Lobster and Fruit."

We noted the shimmering lights, the propensity
of darks. How selectively the artists used white:

the curve of an eggplant, a tipped over candlestick,
in Peale's "Balsam Apple and Vegetables,"

exactly one spot on each glistening red berry-seed
filling the apple's long, crocodile mouth.

With a sweep of your hand, you blessed the page:
"So gorgeous," you said. Then added, "But there's always

this," your mouth going down, eyes lowering,
your finger resting on the image of Chardin's "Silver Tureen,"

with its limp hare, bloodied partridge, and, peering up,
lower left, the hunched tabby ready to pounce.

Japanese Princess

Fingers, the half-moons of your smooth nails
gentle on the bedrail;
my hand on yours, my halting words;
your blue eyes that match the delphiniums rise to meet mine.
You decide you want to walk.
A newspaper slips from the hospital sheets—
flash of the emperor's daughter in street clothes;
her wedding to a commoner,
brave smile for the camera.
I help you get up, put weight on floaty feet;
together we stroll the white halls,
your left hand cupping my upper arm, me
the groom, you the bride. The whole time
your silent eyes flitting to my face, shoulder,
a strap of my sundress, as if
trying to swallow every last crumb,
the way I imagine the princess giving up
her title, royal allowance, wandering a gilt corridor,
studying each polished tile;
finally, how she must have spread wide
the double doors
holding the gold-threaded kingfisher kimono—
glittering, once hers.
        Now, time for me to go, I tuck the blue
and white gown under your legs as you lie down,
pull up sheet, blanket, the weight of flowers.

THE SUICIDE TREES

What if Dante's seventh circle middle
ring stood on its head: the souls of those who
hastened their own deaths turned to trees, sweet,
not brambly and grabby; gentle, generous.

All of them: Vincent, Judy, Sylvia,
Hart, Vachel, Marilyn—Nero, Marc Antony,
Socrates.

Even the less visible—dentist with
a paragraph tucked on the back page of the paper
alive again as an Aspen,

overwhelmed mother, curled in the
shade-drawn house that I unknowingly pedaled
my little green bicycle past—
becomes a Tupelo tree.

Vincent, you would be Almond,
waking after the long night of
white blossoms spilling into grass.

And tall, moonlit Sylvia: a Yew,
of course.

The Romans, I think Walnut,
tree of passion—
or Ash, for ambition.

Judy—Tulip Poplar.

Marilyn, modest Birch.

And dear Michael, late-night boy
who rose at seven for months of Saturdays
to earn a Chicago Botanical Gardens
Master of Trees degree—though you loved
dogwoods, lindens—for you, the Elm.

How you mourned the passing of the beauty
that hugged the brick facade of your century-old

home. "Maybe one more season," the tree surgeon had said—but you knew the ending would not be pretty and spared it a long, unseemly demise.

(Before your body was cremated, we did not "go in back." Now,

I wish I would have touched your foot.)

FREQUENCIES OF BLUE

Three hours later
I arrived at the city
cold and closed as friends
                    in a bad dream
You are on your own now
Ghost words welded my tongue
and where jaw meets ear
a playerless violin tugged taut a sky-blue leash
(longest part of the trip
the fifteen steps from curb
to house
my feet/legs
            stubs)
Beyond the roof lines September pulsed sapphire
straight in front of me
the slow-motion geometries
faces-mouths-plaid shirts
of your awkward country cousins
                    then the wrought lace
of the iron gate
Cool familiars of your garden
eighty-year-old mother's tight-curled round-
shouldered silhouette
weaving among the hostas
Mark's green-and-black checked
sleeves spectacles
lips shaping soft clouds of sound
Endless stream of city friends
words and no words
            am I the only one who hears
that all-but-shattering
E string?

Weeks later
from behind
up over my head
silent vibrato
one and a half decibels
                    pitched
the highest frequency of blue.

QUALIFICATIONS

If it's raining, I will not come.

The sun and moon scrutinize each other. The same.

A fox squirrel turns tail. A white cat on the doorstep.

I accidentally twirl around to the right

and the thunder seems to follow.

I will not come if the soil in the windflower is bone dry.

Absently, I think the word "endodontist" pronounces itself.

The sky looks like snow.

Returning to standard time will make things difficult.

Our little restaurant in the Hotel Burnham

is serving white chocolate banana bread pudding.

Without raisins.

My passport has expired.

By morning, the delicate Grecian bud opens

fourteen pale blue tongues.

First Trip to Chicago After

Children in the First Snow, Paris
gelatin silver print, Edouard Boubat
Art Institute

Scattered jacks on a ghost white
carpet, the children—twelve, fifteen
of them—are half-inch silhouettes
thrust forward, sideways,
back. One boy, bent over at the
waist, elbows parallel to knees,
is a horseshoe.
Hem skirting cold, the girl
in tufted hat squats low
as she can go. Another, down
on one hip, rests his left hand
on something we can't see,
while the right, like Michelangelo's
Adam, fingers eternity.
Explorers landed on a new planet,
engrossed and silent as the aisles
of trees. High branches define the light's
limit. Black arcs of winter-stacked chairs
responding below. The rest—
snow.
        One child, caught mid-
turn, seems momentarily aware
of an observer. Brow raised, mouth
ajar, his wide eyes register surprise—
or, the full measure of being alive.

Friday Afternoon

On top of the comforter (as per my daytime
rules), I read Schuyler's "The Morning of
the Poem" by lamplight, half-aware
of June clouds, pale and slow-dancing.
A brief shower wakens an open screen's
possibilities, in this case a second-floor
sliding door. Behind a bamboo shade,
a floor-to-ceiling scrim of leaves,
thrum of water, color the hour.
The dogs, home from their walk, sleep
on their pillow. Normally, I would be at work.
I turn out the light. All there is breathes.

DIARY

Nearing the end of James Schuyler's diaries,
I fan the corners of the last pages, knowing
there is only a year of intermittent entries left;

I copy one of his tender descriptions of the cat:
Barbara lies stretched against the radiator
as if she has found her long lost mother.

And this quirky weather report: *Deliciously*
overcast, it is the kind of day in August
that makes you think of a day in autumn

which is like a day in winter, everything
simplified. A ghostly apple wedge presses
my throat—I know in six months the diarist

will be dead. The same edge that wakes me from
every Mike-dream, that double-world, where I know
my best friend is going to die—in fact, is already

dead. Yet, just now, here, blond, dreamy-eyed,
he was ordering autumn bulbs for the front garden,
choosing William Morris green-on-cream

sunflower wallpaper for the foyer,
absentmindedly jotting a dinner date—
Jim and Jim—on October's pale blue calendar.

SOME DAYS YOUR DEATH IS SMALL ENOUGH

to fold into a box, decorate with cornets
and rosebuds—shape into a small plate, slide

onto the stack under the hooks and cups.
Antique kimono, botanical print, Louis Sullivan

house. You serving up a slice of latticework
cherry pie. Then, silly-soft, conspiratorial, recounting

the latest egregious faux-pas (accidental fart in yoga class
right as the instructor said, "notice what you smell"),

elbow humor cutting in on the classy waltz
of gardens, wine bars, city boulevards.

Nearly-missed planes, trains, doctors'
appointments. The small anxieties—this shirt,

or that? The large—surgery, now? never?
Ring of trust orbiting your weekly Gilda's Club

(the lovely Venezuelan carefully deflecting
her shaky news: Doctor says, "just a sprinkle,

just a touch"; two months later—gone). Horror,
grief. Then, a slow peace. Mornings made of porcelain.

II.

BEAUTIFUL SHIRTS

Day after Thanksgiving,
no school, parents at work,
turkey and pumpkin still spicing the air,
we sit at your breakfast table
and match shot for shot:
sips from my parents' Friday night
cocktails have taught me a *tiny something*,
but you, raised small-town-protestant-
the-road-to-hell-is-lubricated-with-alcohol,
are pure virgin, and you show it.
Impatient for results, you go straight
for the bottle, each gasp and shudder
marking the rhythm of rip tides to come.
First a jolt, a wheeze,
then a slight spin,
everything starting to curve and blend,
down-shifting, up-shifting,
rocking and tipping,
and before we know it
twenty-four of your grandmother's clover-
leaf rolls have turned to flurries of snow
falling into the green shag carpet,
piling up on the record spinning
on the console, like our faces
in your mother's make-up mirror,
or one of your father's hidden condoms blown
into a balloon. . . . Every moment
so amazing; we even spot a lost pearl
earring among all those crumbs!
Amazing, absolutely amazing.
Then, the beginning of sadness,

the way Daisy cherished Gatsby's clothes
"They're such beautiful shirts.
It makes me sad because I've never seen
such—such beautiful shirts."
And your mother on the phone
pounding fear down like a gavel:
"Boss says I can leave early—see ya soon!"
You ask me to pray at the toilet,
then I jog you barefoot through real snow.
Back in the house, I say, "Slap your face!"
"Sober up!" Meanwhile, your vacuum
chases me down the stairs—I'm pressing
charges. "The nerve," you say, "You're
trying to feed me mud!" and point to
unpercolated coffee settling like fish food
in the bottom of your cup.
We stumble down slushy alleys
towards the anonymity of town, and I know
you see me toss the evidence into
a snowbank a mile from your house,
but all the rest of the day you keep up the litany:
"Where's the Jim Beam? Where's
the Jim Beam?" (*If you ask me
one more time!*), as if words
could lead us back, like bread crumbs.

Post Factum (with Chocolate Cake)

I finally get it: You wanted *always*
to keep doing whatever it was
you were in the middle of
doing; so (by definition) bed-
time, wakeup-time, any *time-
to-do-this, do-that* interrupted:
scritch-scratch of mother-nag.
Evening might find you puttering
around the garden, kitchen, then,
after Mark hits the sack, thumbing through
a stack of clippings looking for that one
recipe (was it the *Times*, or *Gourmet?*)
until you give in and check out
Chez Panisse Desserts, p. 232—
see, you left it marked.
Morning was the pleasure of not
wanting, of slow openings, of
lingering, trying to ignore the back-
ground noise of a lover prepping
for his day in the city. So, it's not
so much you were a Class A
procrastinator—but that you longed
for a stay from endings, a liminal,
in-between, *olly-olly-oxen-free*
zone, no untoward inconvenience
(brain cancer, or death) would jerk
you out of *the now* into *the next*: no
accidental, multiplied factor
of quadruple-decker cake batter
paused, midair, before overrunning
a modest, 3 x 5, lightly-floured plan.

Two Letters

At the service, someone said: "Mike chose joy,"
and you had. You did. *Eventually*. Leafing
through the box of M.J.M. letters, only now
do I really taste the particular alone you once were:
1982: me, married, in Hawaii, you a Chicago CPA
(could there have been a worse mis-match?),
fresh out of college, gay, but not out to me—to
yourself—to anyone: "You've never had a job
you've really hated every minute of," you wrote,
asking forgiveness for your long silence.
"I can't even feel sometimes. I tried to make
myself cry by thinking of the worst thing that
could possibly happen—my parents dying—you
committing suicide—but I couldn't cry."
This, written by hand on the back of some
horrible annual report you'd brought with you
to lovely, lonely French-speaking Quebec.
A week off from your brain-numbing accounting
job, your Near North bachelor apartment.
You didn't meet your first love until 1985, heart
opened to what your body always knew.
Today, I nearly wept (with happiness) on re-finding
your coming-out letter: At the end of a paragraph
lamenting that you and I were not "this instant"
sitting on a low, shady hill with farmland as far
as the eye could see, you quietly announced,
"Two weeks ago, I was introduced to the neatest
person, named Paul Patinka." Your letters, always so
exquisitely explicit: "He told me about his mother's
death. I told him a little about you. We held each
other and we kissed and went upstairs to bed.

It was very sweet. I wasn't able to do anything
sexually, if you know what I mean. I was too
freaked out. After a while, I apologized, told him
if he wanted to go, I would understand. He looked
over and said 'Michael, I'm not going anywhere. . . .'
So we curled up like spoons—on our sides, facing
the same direction, back to stomach. After a while
he fell asleep and I just lay awake the entire night
thinking about him, and you, Jungian analysis,
the Akashic records and God knows what else."

The Day I Made Potato Latkes

It was a breezy June afternoon; it was on-a-lark,
phone-a-travel-agent, catch-the-redeye.

It was hopping the El to the Southport station
and slipping into your and Paul's apartment

with the hidden key. It was tree-shade, napping-till-four,
then waking to mixing bowls—blue, yellow,

red—perched on the ledge next to onions and potatoes.
It was a half-carton of eggs and a skillet.

It was you and Paul strolling in from work,
the first cakes resting on an orange plate.

It was Paul's brown eyes shining, "Hanukkah
in June—I love it." Your Papa-Bear hug

and Peter-Pan grin. It was digging out new candles
for a celebration. It was catching you on the sly

sliding an extra latke onto Paul's plate. It was my quip:
"Are you fattening him up for the slaughter?"

It was a moment of wry laughter.
It was the months before you'd tell me he was HIV

positive—that you'd found out just before my visit—
and when the two of you walked up the steps smelling

onion-laced potatoes you wondered if I knew.
But I was clueless. Blissfully clueless. Now, I wish I could carry

us back, hold us in that summer, sunlight spilling through
linden leaves onto the red-yellow-blue of your kitchen counter.

THANKSGIVING

Chicago cold, leaves rustle brittle wings,
Paul's left hand tucked around
my upper arm,
I feel like an usher at a wedding—
his long navy coat,
the way we pause at each curb
before stepping down.
He is still so handsome.
The three of us headed to your friends'
fashionable apartment.
How Paul's slender fingers struggle
to make out the appetizers
on the coffee table in front of him,
each of us so eager to help transport
a shaky sliver of paté onto a cracker
and up to his mouth.
At dinner ("Thanksgiving is so retro,"
our amiable host set an upbeat tone),
Paul delicately blesses each pile
of food on his plate: broccoli at 3 o'clock,
mashed potatoes at 6, the turkey
someone had cut up for him at high noon.
        Months later, when the two of you
come for a weekend, I turn on every light
in the house. "Forget it," you chide.
"It doesn't do a thing." No-not-a-thing
agrees Paul's shaking head, the setting sun
glinting through the blinds, the dark,
he knows by touch, just in front of him.

Schuyler Yellow

—after a portrait by Fairfield Porter

A love, houseguest, wife's bud
        rolled into one:
Fairfield's palette tips aurelian
        while Jimmy relaxes
In a porch chair. Long-sleeved shirt—
        collar open. Comfy browns:
Hair, pants, sleepy canvas shoes.
        Great Spruce Head seeps
Gray-green through tall screens.
        Not sunny, yet yellow colors
Panels below the screens—grass?
        (maybe). Reminds me of
French's mustard. With mint thrown in.
        Especially compared to Jimmy's
Clean yellow shirt. Tiny triangles
        blessing brow, nose, cheek.
Preppy-slim, pup-shy, pleased-with-
        himself, Jimmy lounges in
His place in this happy
        home. No: in this *home*. Happy
Floats in, lands—departs.
        This afternoon's no different.

A MOODY DAY

Late afternoon, a May day that keeps
revising itself: sun in / out / in. Finally settle
on a book. *A Few Days* (James Schuyler)—
poo-poo-ed by at least
one critic: "he's over-doing it,"
the trope of the la-dee-dah:
here is a flower in a vase, why not
write an ode to it? Oh, and by-the-
bye, I'm listening to Scriabin
(where's the accent in *Scri-a-bin*, anyway?).

The sun pops and I pop out
to a deck chair, open the lush
green summer cover (thank you,
Darragh Park). Jimmy does sing (he's on
the right meds) to snowdrop and velvet rose
and that rose of a girl who takes
care of him (though it's assistant Tom
he has a crush on, he admires Helena's
youth), also, a small "MADE IN ITALY"
notebook—"How it takes me back!"
he sighs and I am taken
to a soft, leather-bound unlined journal
Mike gave me for my birthday—two years
before his death. Five years now—seven

since that b-day (I still remember the black
turtle neck he was wearing—so damn
Aryan). Tightly bound pages
that never worked out. I loved the bury-
your-nose smell, though, and the story

of trudging up a Tuscan hill, partner Mark
in tow, to buy it. Too bad sweet Marcel,
the papillon pup, chewed the wrap-around
leather tie to a crispy point. It was an *objet d'art*
and I let it be mouthed. I felt bad. Then Mike
died. I felt worse. Now, Marcel's dead too.
The day tastes different.

ANYTHING YOU WANT

You've been dead a day.
Before heading downstairs for the night,
Mark said, "Take anything you want."
Shirts, slacks hanging in the closet;
rows of empty shoes, unnameable mist.
On your bookshelf, pale yellow receipt
sticking up from a purple paperback:
Ghost Money.
It would feel like stealing—
living or dead, what's the difference?

My job is to lie in your bed
and keep watch:
2 a.m., I'm gazing up
from your luxurious sheets
through the slatted bedroom doors
at the Fiesta bowls—yellow, orange, ivory, blue—
circling the tops of the kitchen cupboards.

Earlier, I counted earthy ceramic bowls,
ten, twenty . . . on top of the armoire
in the living room.
And in the wide hall from the breakfast nook,
long, low bench of them
alternating, forward and back, close
together, like a child's footsteps.

Above the bench, the rectangular photographs of men.
Groups of men. Boys.
Prep school line-ups. Teammates. Tent mates. Squads.
Broad, chummy grins.

Boys finding their way to each other.
Their mouths were bowls. Their cupped arms.
I tried to recall which clutch of long-lashed fellows
you'd sniffed out in that little shop in Oxford.
A gift for Mark, rolled up, tied
with a ribbon for the long trip home.

THE GIFT

That first night, that last night, when I stayed a-
wake—after your wake—while your partner slept,
I did one tiny thing that might raise
Miss Manners' scrupulous left brow: I slid
open the smallest drawer in your armoire
and found the lily-scented, inscribed French
sachets—dusty pink, antique green—a small
part of what was my last Christmas present
to you. When I'd visited in April
and noted the empty pearl soap dish,
which once held the six one-inch square pillows
(worn-edged—still, they were the heart of the gift),
I almost asked, but did not want to be rude.
I almost asked, *mon ange, mon petit chou.*

SKY IN A JAR

Accept the gift of lavender milk.
Your best friend won't mind. He's dead now.
Though if he were in the next room
it would make him happy to hear the extravagant *wha-sh*
as you tip the entire contents of the pewter jar
into the roiling bath,
the dappled oval of his claw-foot tub.

Step in. Sit down. Lie back.
Let the water swallow your neck.
Dream the little Chapel of the Rosary in Vence
where Matisse convalesced.
Huge yellow-lobed leaves floating up
a Mediterranean sky.

Sit forward: observe how ankles and wrists
separate from the rest, take on a new life.
They remind you of goldfish.
And the child in Mary Cassatt's painting
studying her feet in the bowl of water,
the mother wrapping the towel
around the child's waist.

Now, soak the Egyptian cotton cloth. Wring it once.
Wash your feet, your face, your hands.
Wash the dark, the tenuous.
Wash the place that does not cease to exist
even when the body drifts.

Watch water transpose in the lamp's glow.
Clouds merge, split apart. Decades

pass. The water, the milk,
the measuring spoons.
Two children running through summer.
Dream lavender. Milk in a bottle. Blue in a jar.
Clouds, water, sky; the taste of that color.

BOXES AND BELLS

Upper Slaughter, Lower Slaughter—
Oxfordshire's seesaw of names. Mostly
we stayed on the left-side of things. Parked
the boxy red rental, walked sloping roads
where sheep had passed. That's how sweet
it was. Someone played a bell-song. (You
grinned, "The *Gilligan's Island* theme
would be my only repertoire." We laughed—
the clang of our American-ness.)
Gray evening slipping into the churchyard,
we sat. Unbeknownst to me, more cancer
cells poked around in your blood. You
knew something: "I want to be cremated,
but somewhere . . . a stone."

MIKE

Only you and I would be giddily
in overalls digging out poles with
petrified worms (from the last trip)
still clinging to the hooks, throw it all
into the trunk of your parents' old Impala
and head south without a map, or enough
gas, or any bait. The Tom Sawyer in you
always choosing the long way out of town,
across the tracks where life tasted rougher,
dustier, different. Not just danger and risk—
though that was part of it. Some basic truth;
life ain't gonna be no crystal stair.
Not for a young gay boy. But I didn't know
(1972—you didn't *know*, either).
We just knew people thought we were cousins;
twins. For an entire year, we snorted
like Lily Tomlin's Ernestine. (Pity the poor
teachers who had us together in class.)
Summer days, we'd drive your parents'
car all over hell and gone. No particular route
or destination. Sometimes the Sangamon,
sometimes Kickapoo. Once, the pond in back
of your uncle's farm in Mattoon. Sometimes
we never even made it to water, like the time
we bought cheese and bread and cider at an
Amish farmhouse near Sullivan and chewed
the afternoon away in tall grass. The fishing
was just an excuse to get in the car and travel
where we felt like, to sit in humid air. To be
quiet—but mostly to talk and laugh, to get the
feeling you get after doing that for hours.

Going home had its own ritual, its own
expectations of stopping by Steak 'n Shake
to buy white bags filled with food wrapped
in the same white paper, grease spots spreading
out here and there. Then, food-filled and
exhausted, going the rest of the way home
slumped in self-satisfaction, finally quiet,
but still incredibly wise.

Un Sucrier for Marcel Proust

Not cream. Not white. A small bowl
with a lid, the knob shaped
like a mushroom cap.
The perfect beginning to a young boy's day,
glazed in yarrow light and down the sides,
loose, wide stripes. The whole of it
offset with violet leaf strokes.

Not cream. Not white. But filtered
light in the shadow of trees.
A long table of friends, striped
napkins: a young man momentarily taking
leave of butter knives and wineglasses
to relish the joy of absence.
Shade, and tree-light; fine, charcoal talc.

In a room, in a life, the air waits
for little-boy sighs, little-boy hungers
slipping through the shutters
of a second-floor window, catching
on hawthorn and lilac held
in the night-breeze that flows
over soft currents of the Vivonne
from Combray along the Guermentes Way.

In a room of desire, in a writer's memory,
a stretch of Normandy beach—
young children at the edge, their blue
and white clothes, yellow ribbons.
The sky white, and not white.
Ocean, shore, horizon.

Blue room of hunger, room
of satiation,
world wide as a bowl.
In a room of white-not-white
under a lid, a boy wakes
to reach, not reach.
To sip his mother's *café au lait*
under a pale violet and yellow umbrella.
Feel the stillness, moments poised
on a lip, like the last brimful sentence
of the first page, when he knows *Yes, this*.

III.

In February

"Trees in summer didn't interest Proust"
Jean-Yves Tadié

While the earth is without form, she rises
and wraps herself in French corduroy,
progresses on ballet-feet to the kitchen

where she spoons fresh beans into the grinder,
steels herself for the frenetic. Still,
there is satisfaction in causing such commotion.

The faucet's rush. Enormous, white breakfast
mug. Palpable cool of the metal timer.
She slides her finger under a slip of cheddar

laid out on lavender the evening before. In the distance,
a morning crow calls to his mate, or to the dark,
or to nothing at all. She thinks, *Oh crow, my hidden one,*

you are the sixth degree of something.

PAJAMA PARTY

Reading James Schuyler, late
March, snow gone, mellow
speaker in pajamas (okay,
"undershorts") is enjoying
his morning Maxwell House
(btw: a vintage 60s tin, lid
intact, sells today for ten
dollars—hey, what would
sweet Jimmy make of eBay?
He'd love it, that's what) as he
tunes a *post facto* line to
the shine of maple light,
fat sliver of pages in the *livre
du jour* (some dead dude's
collected letters, I bet)—I,
as a matter, am lounging all
post facto in my aqua pj's
stamped with brimming
white coffee cups, each be-
decked with a pink square—
oops! it's tea, not coffee,
hangs a tag, pink or other-
wise; point is, each cup hosts
two slo-mo squiggles of steam
reminding me of those ashy
snakes we'd light 4 July
(Leaning-Tower-of-Pisa flourishes—
the works) while, inside, deep
bronze invites lips, tongue,
even teeth, as if it's (tags be
damned) *pot de crème* or
Mexican chocolate.

BEECH TREES, LATE AUGUST

Morning
last of last night's rain plunks down
leaf
by leaf
alternating high
then
low
    treble
bass
forests of leaves
a hundred grand pianos of leaves
keyboards skewed
scattershot
view from the window
muted sage
blend of a certain algae-based breakfast drink
(guaranteed
to prolong life)
each moment sliced
silver
not a yellow or gold or brown in sight
nothing here to say
it is not still June, save
the leaves are one shade darker.

Two Flannel Shirts

To slow, let blue
descend to white,

descend to blue,
as when a late summer

evening touches each leaf
of the beech tree,

gathering all
in loose cotton folds,

is to know what Anton Chekhov
knew, two days before his death,

when he sent his wife
to the tailor with instructions

to order two shirts:
one white with a blue stripe,

one blue with a white stripe—
one for now, one for later.

Then beckoned her
to please ask the hotelier

if they might be moved
to a new room.

REFLECTIONS ON THE RUINS OF THE ASYLUM AT SAINT-RÉMY

A strand of ivy scrambles
over the edge
of an empty window,
stray green eighth notes
falling through air
to the cold coda of the floor,
where everything stops,
life coming this far, then *stop*:
slippers, two black stones,
their owner already face-deep
in the tired sheets.

Someone once lay on a bed
and gazed through this window,
measuring time in silent white ships
crossing a linen-blue lake.
But the bars caging the window
could not stop the breeze
from bearing its small gifts:
the scent of blond fields
sleepy with haystacks,
a familiar brown tune
following the grooves
of a slow wagon.

SLEEP

The word used to make me
think *dark*. A black plume.
But last winter, when I rounded
the curve along the inlet,
the pair of swans flew so close,
feathers brushed down the length
of my consciousness,
and I heard their wings say,
white, white, white, white.

ELEGY DRIVING NORTH ON AN INDIANA HIGHWAY

When I headed out of Louisville,
I thought, as I often have these years,
When dark falls, I will be afraid.
At night I see things I can't see by day.

At the northern edge of Indianapolis,
the clouds dissolved into serious black.
Moments later, a clattering of glass when
ghostly pods of Canada geese rose up

from a field, wings pounding air: first *fear*,
then *love*. Liquid, the night appeared
a potion I might drink, or slip into like silk.
The lights of oncoming traffic

were not attached to anything specific.
The glow of a town marked a spot on a map.
I was whole and alone.
In my mind, I said yes, *I can see it all.*

That night I could reckon black wings of
geese, invisible creeks and shadowy trees;
a trunk, a limb, barely knowable things
and your body on that hard shore.

July Days

Last night I used the pink comforter.
This morning, soda-cracker crisp,

I promise my dead
to spend the afternoon doing nothing

save stake out the lake's blue on blue.
Perched on a dune, I get hooked

on a book of Lydia Davis stories:
chuckle out loud over "Letter to a Funeral

Parlor" (*I must say that any portmanteau word,
like* Porta-potty, *or* Pooper-scooper, *has a cheerful,*

*even jovial ring to it that I don't think you intended
when you invented the word* cremains; *however . . .*).

I close my eyes and an imaginary self reads aloud
to an imaginary Mike. I can see him, but not really hear . . .

Summer silence is the loudest.

Piano Before Breakfast

He has a piano that he plays before breakfast. Reminds me
of the guy on the other side of the wall in Mike's apartment

on Wells. When I stayed there alone, every morning, sudden
plink-plink-plonk. Not screaming, but peppy; Bach, Bartok.

Five minutes, less, the wall popped. Then I'd hear the lid
close, the door click open / shut. Mike traveled so much

for his job, he never knew about the next-door maestro
(it was during this period I convinced him, long distance,

that frozen broccoli is better than no broccoli). I wonder
how many people play an instrument

for the last time, knowing, "Okay, this is it—the last time
I will ever hear your voice." Or is it always shrill. Silence.

Days of Clouds

> "This will be hard, so hard, I know. But months and years
> from now you'll see it as the best way."

Long ago and once upon, you did not let the cancer choose
the way for it to end.
Ten years, stealth cells on the march did not keep you from
tree classes, grand travel, ski slopes, tennis matches.
(Still, I stand in a fold of your letter, watch you softly tread those gray stairs.)
      Long ago and once upon, I drove home to friends
who swept my body of rain-torn words. One worried aloud:
A son, who suffers from depression, may one day choose this way, too.
In me snapped a furious string.
Another calmed my heart, my hand: In another place, a culture
frames this *why*, this *when*, with a different noun,
different verb; different way to use a word.

Why It Pisses Me Off When Someone Assumes You Died of AIDS

Because too many times
the boot heel of everyday

hatred drives its spike
into the gullet and gut of

what matters to me most.
Because you died of everyday,

socially acceptable cancer.
Because you weren't HIV-positive;

because it doesn't matter.
Because it does matter

that people check their assumptions.
Because I've seen someone

who's sat at my table
say *gay people*, look

down in shame
and in that look

murder thousands.
Because in my long-

enough, straight and pink-
tinged-white life

I have not done enough
and this poem

won't erase that.

The Café of Our Departure

Near the *sous-sol* of our lives, where nothing sacred
escapes, there is a room where no one goes

of their own accord.
Yet, eventually, a crowd gathers.

One by one, we descend from terrace tables
in search of our dearest friend

who unbuttoned his shirt, laid out
the wild daisy of his life.

The cancer so slow no chemo would touch it;
so rare.

Now, in the *sous-sol* of our grief, we do not weep.
And then we weep.

Days dreamt in scrim of terrace clatter. Forkfuls
of lemon cake. While one street away

silent silhouettes stroll, flowers gray and
no rain catches. Gravity turns, and turns us.

How will we do this?
Life is the one house where someone knew us.

Seven Months Later

We are standing in the half-light
of an everyday room—
maybe a hallway to a kitchen—
and I am telling you about some large-scale
sadness; a war, the diminished lives
of an oppressed people.

You smile
the smile of someone who knows he knows
something you don't know
but who loves you
and does not lord it over you.

You're going to kill yourself.
And there is that terrible moment
poised on the head of a pin,
when I know, out of love, out of respect—
out of powerlessness—the-room-inside-
a-dream-room
that separates us all,
I will let you.

ANHEDONIA AT BROOKFIELD, 2008

In the Kingdom of the Apes, Dean and I sigh
over an infant orangutan's *almost-not-there* finger
    feathering its mother's chin; tiny balds

    camouflaged against a nipple. In my pocket,
murmur of darks—Pat's intimate, chiseled bird-script
    mailed from Manoa (decades it's been since

    our paths crossed at the university): "Colt" died
eleven months ago and though she *yogas* and walks
    and swims, nothing takes her out

    or in. She misses the tickle, the incense of him.
(She has this word for it.) Five years my Mike's been gone—
    gay-boy blue, soul-mate since ninth grade.

    1971, the studies had not yet been done ("Gay Men,
Straight Women Have Similar Brains"); we didn't have
    a word for it; in each other's pockets, we rollicked

    our way through school, and ever-after. Mike,
blond, long-lashed. Pat's eyes, so deep they felt black. Dean's,
    brown with gold sparks that match his hair

    (Dean's dad—angry man—once said:
"Your eyes look like dog turds floating in a bowl of milk."
    How does a child erase a sting like that?).

    We are called to love the staggering hurt in everyone.
Some days, all my dears are circling the Serengeti, languid
    as young giraffes, all tongue and munch

swaying from tree to tree, for no reason than the stroll
of it. Oh, M., since your death, I still look forward to every
breakfast, but what I miss these weeks, years

since you bravely (absolutely) ended
your cancer-suffering with your own hand. Part
of me; frozen, waiting for a different

phone ring. When I stumble—as we
were wont to do—on something so heroically
hilarious it demands to be shared: that perfect

purple shoe fits only you. Not Pat's loss, not
Dean's pain; the absence of you, ever-nascent:
mine to name.

VIOLETS FOR MANET

Not only the fan, and the woman in the long dress
unfolding in liquid intervals, but the small blue flowers
tied together at the waist,

and the sound of someone returning in the dark,
the mouth slightly open, eyes dreamy
and relaxed;

nothing foreshadowed.
Only echoes dispensed
down a long hall, a door opening, closing,

and not only the elegant, handwritten invitation,
creased and wizened, but a creamy custard
inscribed with chocolate epigraphs.

The clock, the orange cat, each individual blossom—
the entire house—pulsing.
The sleeping, syphilitic painter, the amputated leg . . .

Not only the woman who has walked away
from her flowers and fan, but the subject
and desire, the hidden hem,

and the memory of sheer texture curtaining
the cradle, the blur of faces
disembarking from a ship. If someone

loosens the ribbon, dulls the fever,
opens a window to the sound of rain, then the artist
may rise to his task: the lovely pieces of shattered glass.

Two Rooms

One for bluebirds, one for crows.

One to sleep in.
One to air.

One for shadow, one for snow.

One for noise;
one for color.

One for poems—one for hats.

One for Veuve Clicquot; one for ash.

One for butter cookies.
One for a clock.

One to polish, one to lock.

One to listen . . . one to knock.

One for orange water.
One for a bitter leaf.

One to empty, one to fill.

THE BOY WHO LOVED BUTTERFLIES
for T.

Though sunlight spills in from the playground,
the clank and clamor of other children,
he falls into the silence of wings.
Every morning he falls into them
the way he fell out of his mother
into the dusty blue iridescence.
Now, he is in the corner with his book,
his one good hand stroking velvet
colors, the scalloped yellow edge
of a mourning cloak.
He prefers the dorsal view,
the bright-colored fur and jungle-eyed
wings of swallowtails.
He carefully measures beauty
with his flattened palm.
Later, he asks the French teacher
for a new word: "*Papillon*,"
she whispers.
"*Papillon de nuit*, for moth.
Papillons noirs means gloomy thoughts.
If I say, '*Chasse tes papillons noirs*,'
it means you will be happy again."

THE CAFÉ OF OUR
DEPARTURE

ACKNOWLEDGMENTS & NOTES

My deep appreciation to my poetry buddies, whose intelligence and care have helped immeasurably in the creation of this book. Jackie Bartley, you are the mother lode; you opened the door to your yellow house and welcomed me (and my wad of poems). Laura Donnelly and Ralph Hamilton, your brilliant, close readings made the difference. Also, appreciation to the late Rane Arroyo, and to Jane Bach, Kristin Brace, Debra Kang Dean, David James, Kathleen McGookey, Maureen Moorehead, Rosanne Osborne, Greg Pape, Molly Peacock, Greg Rappleye, Jack Ridl, Peter Schakel, Heather Sellers, and Debra Wierenga, who have all taught me and touched this manuscript in some way. Jack and Jane, for letting me weep, and still doing the "work." Heather, for the evening you said "give him a book." Kathi, your savvy tweak let something "click" *parfaitement* into place. The list of friends and good colleagues who have brought light to my life and my writing would fill up two pages. Bryan Borland, Seth Pennington, and Sarah Rawlinson at Sibling Rivalry Press: you were the perfect ones: Thank you.

My love to Dean, especially, who makes home *home*, to Jackie, who makes Holland home, to hanai daughter Becky, and to my siblings (unrivaled), without whom I would not be: Lee, Kurt, Margaret, and especially Lynn, to whom, along with her partner Marylee, this book is dedicated.

Many thanks to the editors of the following journals, where many of these poems first appeared:

Antiphon: "A Moody Day."
Assisi: "Two Rooms."
Bananafish: "July Days."
Blast Furnace: "Mike."
CANT: "Unguided Tour of Grief with Green Wallpaper."
Center: "Two Flannel Shirts."
Chiron Review: "Beautiful Shirts."
The Dalhousie Review: "The Gift."
Digital Papercut: "Days of Clouds."
Dirty Napkin: "Post Factum (with Chocolate Cake)."
The Dos Passos Review: "Two Letters."
The Fourth River: "Some Days Your Death Is Small
        Enough."
The Great American Literary Magazine: "Pajama Party."
Heavy Feather Review: "Anything You Want," "Japanese
        Princess."
Illuminations: "Qualifications."
Jelly Bucket: "Elegy Driving North on an Indiana
        Highway."
Juked: "Boxes and Bells," "Seven Months Later."
The Louisville Review: "Sky in a Jar," "The Suicide Trees."
The Midwest Quarterly: "Beech Trees, Late August," "In
        February," "Sleep."
Natural Bridge: "Thanksgiving."
The New Poet: "Hospitals & Guns."
Poetry: "Reflections on the Ruins of the Asylum at Saint-
        Rémy."
Poetry London: "The Day I Made Potato Latkes."
Scapegoat: "Diary."
Southern Humanities Review: "First Trip to Chicago,
        After" (under the title "Children in the First
        Snow, Paris"), *La Nature Morte*, *Un Sucrier* for
        Marcel Proust."

The Southern Review: "Violets for Manet."

Superstition Review: "Piano Before Breakfast."

Sycamore Review: "Cabinet of Wonder."

The William and Mary Review: "The Boy Who Loved Butterflies."

Water~Stone: "The Café of Our Departure."

Womb Poetry: "Frequencies of Blue."

"The Boy Who Loved Butterflies" was reprinted in *New Poems from the Third Coast: Contemporary Michigan Poetry* (Detroit: Wayne State University Press, 2000).

"Prince of the City" is the title of a painting by Lee Godie.

About the Author

Priscilla Atkins, born and raised in Central Illinois, attended college in Massachusetts, lived in Southern California for one year, and in Hawaii for ten. She received her MFA from Spalding University. She resides in Michigan amidst a swirl of beech trees with two small dogs and a tall man.

About the Press

Sibling Rivalry Press is an independent publishing house based in Little Rock, Arkansas. Our mission is to publish work that disturbs and enraptures.

www.siblingrivalrypress.com

Gratitude

This book was produced, in part, due to the support of the non-profit Sibling Rivalry Press Foundation. The Sibling Rivalry Press Foundation assists small presses and small press authors through grants and fiscal sponsorship.

www.srpfoundation.org

CPSIA information can be obtained at www.ICGtesting.com
Printed in the USA
LVOW12s0026200215

427592LV00005B/103/P